THE GREAT MASTERS OF DRAWING

DRAWINGS BY

LEONARDO DA VINCI

BY

GIORGIO CASTELFRANCO

TRANSLATED BY

FLORENCE H. PHILLIPS

SECOND ENLARGED EDITION

DOVER PUBLICATIONS, INC., NEW YORK

Published in Canada by
GENERAL PUBLISHING COMPANY, LTD.
30 LESMILL ROAD, DON MILLS, TORONTO, ONTARIO.

Leonardo da Vinci is a new translation, first published by Dover Publications, Inc., in 1968, of the work *Leonardo* first published by Aldo Martello, Milan, 1965, in his series "I Grandi Maestri del Disegno." The present edition, which contains all the original illustrations, is published by special arrangement with Mr. Martello.

Second enlarged edition, first published in 1971, contains a Supplement of 30 additional illustrations selected from *The Drawings of the Florentine Painters* by Bernhard Berenson (1903) and *The Notebooks of Leonardo da Vinci* edited by Jean Paul Richter (1883; Dover reprint, 1970).

International Standard Book Number: 0-486-21945-3
Library of Congress Catalog Card Number: 67-25595

Manufactured in the United States of America

DOVER PUBLICATIONS, INC.
180 VARICK STREET, NEW YORK, N. Y. 10014

LEONARDO'S DRAWINGS

IF one were to ask why Leonardo da Vinci drew as much as he did throughout his entire life, and why he did so with such personal delight, such insistence, such a fever of inventiveness and such extraordinary results, one would find oneself considering all the explanations which have been given and which it seems possible to give, and finally returning to a single, self-evident, extremely simple answer: Leonardo drew because he was a draughtsman; that is, he felt able to express himself fully in the two-color pictorial medium which we call "drawing." Except for the occasional modest introduction of other subsidiary colors, drawing is, in effect, a way of painting which uses the paper itself to achieve light, and which employs pen, pencil, silverpoint, sanguine or any graphic medium whatsoever for shadow. It is a pictorial art which basically refuses to vie with the multiplicity of colors in the real world.

If one then asks how drawing can so often succeed in expressing man's deepest and most poetic emotions, when one would think that the firm renunciation of the reality of color would cut an artist off from basic contact with the world—then the answer is anything but simple. On the one hand, it goes without saying that the infinite variety of colors in the objective, real world is virtually impossible to reproduce; thus, even when an artist proposes to "paint reality" he is always forced to simplify enormously, reducing nature to those relatively few colors which he can create in paint, and which best seem to compose an image out of the whole complex of stimuli he has received from the objects before him. In other words, he must choose, or rather fashion, a combination of colors which fundamentally he himself has invented.

Then, on the other hand, one must bear in mind that man's natural tendency is to condense the external realities of color by subjectively and selectively interpreting the colors of any given object in terms of their visual impact: that is, according to the degree of light or darkness involved in what is seen.

I

Out of all this comes that intrinsically non-chromatic image which is commonly called the "form" of things. And one must not lose sight of the fact that man is far more apt to remember form than color, both because forms change much less than colors at different hours of the day and in different illuminations, and because they provide things with those fundamental structural attributes which no one can possibly ignore if he hopes to live and function in the world.

To depict life in the black-and-white medium of drawing is therefore anything but contrary to the norms of man's visual nature.

It is also true that because drawing does away with the chromatic aspects of individual objects, it tends to invest them with a generic quality, as is evidenced by the fact that drawing and its derivative, the monochrome print, have always seemed the most obvious media for scientific illustration of types: animal and vegetable species, geological formations and so on.

Furthermore, given the great rapidity and convenience of drawing as opposed to painting of any kind, it has always lent itself admirably to painters' and sculptors' first attempts at setting down their ideas, testing structural values, adapting elements from previous works to new compositions or experimenting with typical, generic forms before trying to individualize them and gradually absorb them into a personal style.

In presenting this small sampling of Leonardo's drawings, I would like to begin by clearing up one misunderstanding which often arises because he devoted so much of his energies to the natural sciences. The technical, categorical type of drawing of which science has made extensive use both before and especially since his lifetime was never the prevalent type in Leonardo's production. Impersonal drawings which do no more than set down some specific piece of information are exceedingly rare in the total body of his work

Leonardo—and this he expressed clearly in his writings, as well as giving visual evidence of it in his pictorial works—believed in nature. He believed in an objective natural reality, rational and knowable, but he most emphatically did not consider this reality to be a static order; to him it was the creative impulse inherent in nature. This made him consider every natural object and organism from the standpoint of its intrinsic vital energies, so that his imagination immediately rendered anything he saw unique and individual. In animals, it was physical structure which interested him because the creatures' physical structure so clearly suited them for movement and action—specifically their own action, generated by their own volition. Rocks, water, rivers fascinated him because they were the products of millennial operations of geological forces; plants, because there was such order in the pattern of their growth, in the disposition of their organs, in their relationships with the other elements and energies of the world. Whether he was drawing horses (in preparation of his monumental statue of Francesco Sforza, or of *The Battle of Anghiari*) or cats (for *The Madonna of the Cat*, which he never painted) or a monkey, or any other animal, he always endowed them with individuality and some particular drama of their own: perhaps the drama of bestiality, or crazed abandon, or domesticated cunning. When he studied stratifications in the rocky Lombard foothills of the Alps, he was seeking to recreate in his picture the geological forces which had thrown up such jagged layers of rock, and the storms which had so battered and eroded them. Then there was the light on the poplar grove, that light which he explained so well (though Galileo, admittedly, would have explained it better): "Wherever trees, or rather their branches, grow more densely, there it is darker because the air cannot penetrate; but wherever the branches stand out clearly above one another, there the areas of light are brighter, and the leaves are lustrous because the sun illuminates them."

Even when Leonardo undertook complex and more or less traditional subject matter, he brought the demands of a poetic imagination to bear upon it from the earliest stages of the work. It is extremely rare to find him drawing forms vaguely or approximatively, and the sketches for *The Madonna of the Cat* and *The Madonna with the Fruit Dish* which we include here

(Plates 6 and 7) are only random examples, among many, of this initial simultaneity of his imagination and gesture. It was an imagination which could conceive forms of extraordinary nobility and beauty, while the artistic gesture which served as their vehicle is still as touching in its lyricism as it was rapid in execution. We see each of the pages just mentioned as one unified, self-contained and self-propelling arabesque, which pauses to define the lines and masses of the subject, but which most of all conveys, intact, a glimpse of an entire poetic of form, vast in its sweep, and endless in the continuity of its tension: the product of a few moments of absolute graphic felicity.

Again and again, and always with the greatest creative intensity, Leonardo experimented with themes which he intended to use in paintings or sculptures, but he also often, as in these two drawings, simply tried out subjects which fascinated him, without aiming at any eventual major work. He continually took great pains to create and recreate the characters of the large compositions for which he had received commissions, but then too he would draw human figures simply because he found them beautiful, noble, typical. Sometimes he delved for human types among his distant personal memories, and then adapted them to fantastic dramas of his own invention. His fascination with natural forms and phenomena led him to draw sometimes from life, with strict devotion to the subtlest realistic detail, and sometimes from memory, expanding and adapting his subject to fit his own conception of nature as the perennial destroyer and the perennial creator of new forms. His sense of structure lent reality to his most fantastic drawings of invented weapons, invented battles, allegories and even (for he was a *homo inter homines*) theatrical subjects, and by the same token he endowed each of his studies of human and animal anatomy with a vivid sense of life and individuality. Drawing was his native tongue; through drawing he seemed to be able to crystallize and express everything he thought, for he seems always to have thought in visual terms. The corpus of his drawings thus not only represents the collected drawings of a great painter, but is also a great pictorial diary. It is like an immense archive in which he set down, with maximum expressive tension, all the figurative facts, as it were, of his life— a life dedicated with unparalleled energy to investigating the essence of form in the universe.

It would be foolish to try to make a general distinction between Leonardo's preparatory drawings for large works and drawings which he did for their own sake, because he was naturally inclined to bring to any new work, whether in painting or drawing, forms and motifs which he had already studied and worked out. As an example of the persistence of certain types we would like to point out that the head of a soft-featured adolescent boy on the recto of folio 12276 of the Windsor Castle drawings, dated about 1475 (Plate 4), is already repeated at the upper left of the very same page, slightly modified, as a female head. On the verso of the same sheet it appears on the body of a young woman, almost as though it were a portrait. Then in subsequent years Leonardo repeated it innumerable times, so that we even find it on a page of the *Second Book of Anatomy*, which is one of his latest manuscripts. Nor should we fail to mention the strong similarity between this head and that of the angel in Verrocchio's *Baptism of Christ* in the Uffizi, which according to Vasari was a contribution by the "youth" Leonardo to that painting. The old man's head which appears near the boy's on our same page of drawings (Plate 4) has an even longer history of recurrence. Other examples which immediately come to mind include the Madonna of the Uffizi *Adoration of the Magi*, who is based on studies for *The Madonna of the Cat*; the shapes and movements of the horses in *The Battle of Anghiari*, which are taken from the *Adoration* painted more than twenty years earlier; and so forth.

In certain of Leonardo's drawings there are elements of form and light which have direct bearing on his paintings, but others, particularly the Lombardy landscape drawings, go beyond the paintings. There is an essential structural articulation and a quality of movement in the light in these drawings which makes it difficult to associate them with the marvelous but "distant" backgrounds of the *Mona Lisa* or *The Virgin with Saint Anne*. Similarly, the caricature study of five heads (Plate 15) is drawn with a ruthless precision in the line and a brightness in the forms which never occur in Leonardo's canvases, and which really herald the development of the "grotesque" in northern European painting of the sixteenth century. Finally, Leonardo's drawings of strange weapons and armed men, the movement of the figures executed with lightning rapidity of line, are not matched by anything in his painting; nor are certain of his tiny scenes and allegories, suffused with clear light, drawn with a great feeling for illusion, as chatty as a tale and yet as self-contained as medallions.

If we move, then, from Leonardo's few though remarkable paintings to a study of his drawings, we find that his artistic world, while perhaps not grander, certainly seems to become far more varied.

Leonardo's graphic techniques were also extremely varied: pen alone, pen and brush, silverpoint, black crayon or sanguine, often with brushstroke additions of white-lead high-lighting. And while his styles of drawing were equally diversified, we cannot really say that there was any clear progression in time from one style to another; in general he incorporated the new with the old. Without any claim to a complete or definitive categorization, however, we can offer the following approximate chronological arrangement of his graphic styles: pure contour drawing; drawing wherein the contours are strongly marked, with shadows created by slanted, distinct, parallel lines, like those seen in many engravings of the period; drawing wherein the contours are less marked and the shadows, while still done in line, are deepened here and there with dark touches. These styles of drawing, all already employed during Leonardo's first Florentine period (until about 1482), are complemented by another style, more interior in quality and with very little shading, in which the lines rapidly indicate the body's musculature and intimate structure, rather than following its contours. From the first Milanese period (from about 1482 to 1500) there are many drawings executed with great finish, in which effects of light are minutely thought out and the chiaroscuro extremely gradated so as to absorb completely delineation and contours. Examples of this are the cartoon for *The Virgin with Saint Anne* (Plate 20) and, slightly later in date, the studies of heads for *The Battle of Anghiari* (Plate 27). But Leonardo's pen still remains evident in the calligraphy of his landscapes, defining mountains, rocks, rivers; sometimes used in isolation to bring out geological anatomy, sometimes with a subtle line freely interwoven in it—compact in one place, in another almost grainy with light—to give the feeling of reflections in water, spaces between leaves or airy distant expanses.

How much did Leonardo's devotion to draughtsmanship owe to his Florentine schooling, and to what extent did it simply arise out of his own talent? Certainly Verrocchio and Pollaiuolo, the Renaissance masters closest to Leonardo, were seriously exploring the structural manifestation of form as a function especially of movement and Pollaiuolo even more than Verrocchio employed lines which swiftly delineated the internal structure of bodies—a style of drawing which Leonardo very soon took up himself. But Leonardo's renunciation of the variety of colors in nature was a more conscious choice than it had been for his predecessors and could already be seen in the first documented decade of his work. Right from the start he tended to fuse all the anatomical components of a figure through extremely gradated modeling, keeping light and shadow in melodic tension, and allowing himself no sudden transitions or omissions. It was this Leonardesque quality of "nuance" (*sfumato*) which enabled drawing to approach the level of painting, and any limitations which the medium imposed on the artist were more than compensated by the possibility of rapidity and technical ease.

Then, to repeat, Leonardo's mentality was directed above all toward an art which would interpret—not imitate—nature; an art which would be valid to the extent that the created image was an extension of and in harmony with the essential creative Logos of the world. Thus the artist's daily objective became mastery of the structure of things—a structure simultaneously lyrical and rational. And in order to set down this structure in a figurative world expanding miraculously with ever greater felicity, drawing became his unsurpassable medium for a life's work that was to be unceasing, proceeding *de claritate ad claritatem* until his last days.

One final word on the vicissitudes of Leonardo's drawings. For the most part, they are now in Windsor Castle as the property of the royal house of England; this is due to an unfortunate chapter in the annals of Italian art collecting. Leonardo made Francesco Melzi, his Milanese pupil, heir to his notebooks, drawings, models and other similar items; but while Melzi considered them precious "as relics," he apparently made no effort during his long life to have them adequately publicized and appreciated. When Francesco died in 1570, Orazio Melzi, out of ignorance rather than need, for he was a weathly nobleman, distributed them to various people. A large part went to Pompeo Leoni, a sculptor at the court of Madrid, who then sold the anatomy books and a large number of drawings to Don Juan de Espina, from whom Thomas Howard Arundel acquired them about 1640. From Lord Arundel, who was a cultured man, a collector of antiquities and a connoisseur of things Italian, the drawings passed into the English royal collections; the year of this transfer is uncertain.

The groups of Leonardo drawings owned by the British Museum, the Louvre, the Uffizi, the Accademia in Venice, the Biblioteca Reale (Royal Library) in Turin and other collections are all far smaller than the Windsor Castle collection.

However, the drawings which survive undoubtedly represent only a fraction of what Leonardo actually produced. Above all, his cartoons have been lost, except one for *The Virgin with Saint Anne* and one for a portrait of Isabella d'Este which he never painted. It is incredible to think that we have no preliminary drawings for the *Mona Lisa*; that we can count on our fingers the drawings for *The Last Supper*, for which Leonardo must have made the most laborious preparations; and that for *The Virgin of the Rocks* (the first version, in the Louvre) perhaps the only preliminary drawing we have is the head of the angel (Plate 12), since the very few others that exist seem to be for the copy of the painting in the National Gallery in London. We can assume that this dispersion of the drawings occurred partly during Leonardo's own lifetime, for in Renaissance studios drawings were considered working tools, not collector's items, and Leonardo's greatest personal concern was bound to have been his anatomical drawings or at any rate those of scientific content. But there is no doubt that the years during which the drawings were in Orazio Melzi's hands were the truly calamitous years. In the words of Giovanni Ambrogio Mazenta: "Many people went to this Dr. Melzi and sought drawings, models, sculptures, anatomical studies...." Finally, we have the certain knowledge that nearly a quarter of the Windsor Castle drawings have been lost, for at the time of George III they numbered seven hundred seventy-nine, while now there are only about six hundred.

In brief, Fate, which has never been kind to Leonardo's work, has not even spared his drawings; but we really cannot spend time in regret, because his achievement in this field was such that it has survived in spectacular richness and vitality to our own day.

A BRIEF CHRONOLOGY

1452 (April 15): Leonardo born at Vinci, the natural son of Ser Piero, a notary.

FIRST FLORENTINE PERIOD

1469 Leonardo's family was in Florence; Leonardo probably already in the workshop of Andrea del Verrocchio.

1476 Still in the workshop of Andrea del Verrocchio.

1481 Payment made for *The Adoration of the Magi*, now in the Uffizi.

FIRST MILANESE PERIOD

1483 Contract for *The Virgin of the Rocks*, now in the Louvre.

1490 Resumes work on the monument to Francesco Sforza.

1497 *The Last Supper*, in the refectory of Santa Maria delle Grazie, already well under way.

1499 (December): Leaves Milan, which has been occupied by the French. The mould of the monument to Francesco Sforza, finished but not yet cast in bronze, is damaged. Vain attempts to acquire it, two years later, on the part of the Duke of Ferrara, Ercole I (it was destroyed).

SECOND FLORENTINE PERIOD

1500 (April 24): Arrives in Florence.

1501 Cartoon for *The Virgin with Saint Anne*, now in the Louvre.

1503–1504 Cartoon for *The Battle of Anghiari*.

1505 Commencement of the painting of *The Battle of Anghiari* in the Council Hall (Sala del Consiglio) of the Palazzo Vecchio. Technical problems lead to abandonment of the work (destroyed shortly after the middle of the sixteenth century).

SECOND MILANESE PERIOD

1506–1513 At Milan, except for long stays in Florence.

1513 (autumn): Leonardo leaves for Rome.

ROMAN PERIOD

1513–1516 In the service of Giuliano de' Medici, the nephew of Leo X. Last documentation of Leonardo in Rome is August 1516.

FRENCH PERIOD

1516–1519 Leonardo lives in Cloux, near Amboise.

1519 (April 23): Writes his will.

1519 (May 2): Leonardo dies in the Château de Cloux.

PRINCIPAL WORKS ON THE DRAWINGS OF LEONARDO

I manoscritti e i disegni di Leonardo da Vinci pubblicati dalla Commissione Vinciana; Disegni. Six volumes, published between 1928 and 1948, with text and notes by Adolfo Venturi. A basic work for any study of Leonardo's drawings, especially because of the perfection of the facsimile reproductions. A seventh volume is now being published which includes several late drawings not published in Vol. VI for technical reasons, also transcriptions, indexes, etc.

BERENSON, B.
The Drawings of the Florentine Painters, University of Chicago Press, 1938. Second edition, containing important additions, especially in the section about Leonardo, of the work first published in 1903.

BODMER, H.
Leonardo, Stuttgart, 1931. This is Vol. 37 of *Klassiker der Kunst,* and is largely devoted to Leonardo's drawings.

CLARK, K.
A Catalogue of the Drawings of Leonardo da Vinci in the Collection of H. M. the King at Windsor Castle, Cambridge, 1935. A scholarly and extremely accurate catalogue of the Windsor Castle collection, by far the most important collection.

POPHAM, A. E.
The Drawings of Leonardo da Vinci, New York, 1945; Brussels, 1947. Reproduces 320 of Leonardo's drawings; the most substantial recent work on the subject.

POPHAM, A. E., AND POUNCEY, P.
Italian Drawings in the British Museum, London, 1950. Pages 56–76 are devoted to the 33 sheets of Leonardo drawings, and provide extremely up-to-date information on the subject.

POPP, A. E.
Leonardo da Vinci, Zeichnungen, Munich, 1928.

VERGA, E.
Bibliografia Vinciana, Bologna, 1931. Contains bibliographical information on and summaries of 2900 (!) writings by and about Leonardo up to and including 1930. Essential for Leonardo studies.

For other information see the bibliographies of the articles "Leonardo" in the *Enciclopedia Italiana,* Vol. XX, 1933, and the *Enciclopedia Cattolica,* Vol. VII, 1951.

LIST OF PLATES

1. Landscape

2. Study of drapery

3. Head of a woman

4. Diverse figures, and a sketch for a *Madonna with the Christ Child and the Child Saint John the Baptist*

5. (*a*) Infantrymen with new weapons against lancers

    (*b*) Head of an old man and profile of a youth

6. Studies for a *Madonna of the Cat*

7. Madonna and Child (with a fruit dish)

8. Studies for a bust of a woman

9. Studies for an *Adoration of the Shepherds*

10. Over-all study for *The Adoration of the Magi*

11. Allegory

12. Study for the angel's head in *The Virgin of the Rocks*

13. Catapult

14. Cannon foundry

15. Old man with a wreath of oak leaves, surrounded by four grotesque figures

16. Study of horses

17. Bust of a man, and an architectural study

18. Earthquake, fiery rain, resurrection of the dead, and other studies

19. Cartoon for *The Virgin with Saint Anne*

20. Head for the Saint Anne in *The Virgin with Saint Anne*

21. Plant study: *Sparganium erectum L.*

22. Plant study: *Rubus Idaeus L.*

23. Plant study: *Coix Lachryma L.*

24. (*a*) Horse and rider

    (*b and c*) Battle sketches for *The Battle of Anghiari*

25. Horses

26. Study of horses, and head of a shouting man

27. Head of a young man

28. (*a*) Poplar grove

    (*b*) Rope-drawn ferry

29. Storm in the mountains

30. Study of rocks

31. Design for Marshal Trivulzio's tomb monument

32. Cataclysm

SUPPLEMENT

33. Sketch for the hanging figure of Bernardo di Bandino

34. Studies for a *Madonna of the Cat*

35. Bust of a warrior

36. Studies of an angel placing a shield on a trophy and separate studies of an angel

37. Study of the perspective of the background of *The Adoration of the Magi*

38. Allegorical composition

39. The proportions of the human figure

40. Profile of a lady

41. Nude on horseback trampling a prostrate foe

42. Studies for the Sforza monument

43. Design for a stable

44. Architectural drawing

45. Sketch for the laying out of a town

46. Plan for a church

47. The unmasking of evil

48. Sketch for an allegory

49. Head of a man

50. Head of a man

51. Preparatory sketch for the painting of *The Last Supper*

52. Study of female hands

53. Study of drapery

54. Studies of the head of Cesare Borgia

55. Warriors' heads

56. Neptune guiding his sea horses

57. Study from the antique

58. Studies of dancing nymphs

59. Studies of the head and shoulders of a man

60. Allegory

61. Youth with a lance

62. Sketches for a kneeling Leda and a horse

1. *Landscape.* The inscription reads: "di S. Maria della neve addì 5 d'agosto 1473" (of St. Mary of the Snow, August 5, 1473). First undisputed work by Leonardo. Pen. *(Florence, Uffizi, #8.)*

2. *Study of drapery.* Generally held to be a work from Leonardo's first Florentine period.
Bistre on canvas, with white lead. *(Paris, Louvre, #2255.)*

3. *Head of a woman.* Though not unanimously attributed to Leonardo, this drawing is
faithfully followed in the Louvre *Annunciation* and was probably executed about 1475. Pen
and white lead. The whites, however; have been retouched on the face and throat.

(Florence, Uffizi, #428.)

4. *Diverse figures, and a sketch for a "Madonna with the Christ Child and the Child St. John the Baptist."* About 1475. Pen. *(Windsor, #12276 r.)*

5(a). *Infantrymen with new weapons against lancers.* First half of the first Milanese period.
(Venice, Accademia, #235 r.)

5(b). *Head of an old man and profile of a youth.* The note reads: "bre 14/8 mcnommciai
le 2 Vergine Marie" (...ber 1478 [thus, in the last months of 1478] I began the two Virgins).
Pen. *(Florence, Uffizi #446.)*

6. *Studies for a "Madonna of the Cat."* A subject which Leonardo also studied in nine other
known drawings. About 1480. Pen. *(London, British Museum, 1860, 6, 16, 98 r.)*

7. *Madonna and Child* (with a fruit dish). About 1480. Pen and silverpoint.
(Paris, Louvre, R.F. 486.)

8. *Studies for a bust of a woman.* About 1480. Silverpoint. *(Windsor, #12513.)*

9. *Studies for an Adoration of the Shepherds.* About 1480. Pen.
(Bayonne, Musée Bonnat, #658.)

10. *Over-all study for "The Adoration of the Magi."* The composition and the figures were later considerably modified in the Uffizi painting. About 1481. Pen. *(Paris, Louvre, #1978.)*

11. *Allegory*. The figure on the right with the child in its arms is Fortune. The youth with the torch is Death; he is being supported by Pride and Ignorance. This is according to the now barely legible names inscribed on the drawing. However, the allegorical meaning is not clear. On the back of the sheet are figures for *The Adoration of the Magi*, which would place it about 1481 or shortly afterward. Silverpoint and pen. *(London, British Museum, 1886, 6, 9, 42.)*

12. *Study for the angel's head in "The Virgin of the Rocks."* Dated as 1483. The model was probably a young girl. This is among Leonardo's most polished drawings. Silverpoint. *(Turin, Biblioteca Reale, #15572.)*

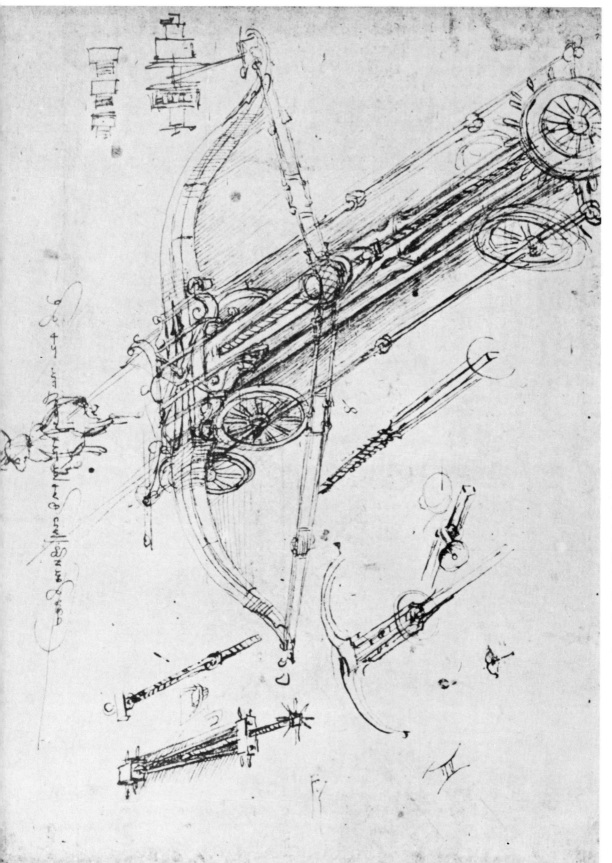

13. *Catapult.* First half of the first Milanese period. Pen. *(Milan, Biblioteca Ambrosiana, Codice Atlantico, fol. 52, v. a.)*

14. *Cannon foundry.* About 1490. Pen. *(Windsor, #12647.)*

15. *Old man with a wreath of oak leaves, surrounded by four grotesque figures.* Last years
of the first Milanese period. Pen. *(Windsor, #12495.)*

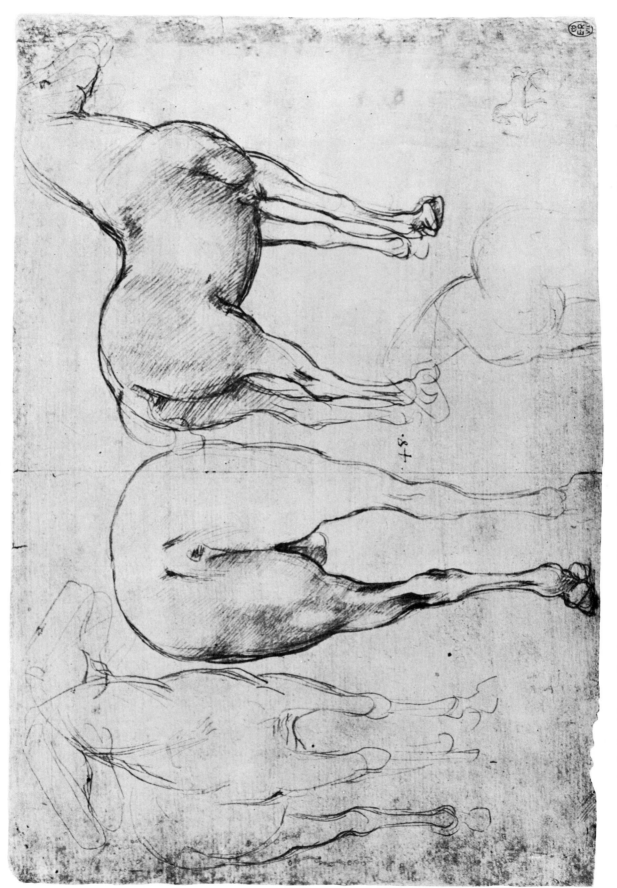

16. *Study of horses.* For the monument to Francesco Sforza. The small horse at the bottom right shows the plan which Leonardo eventually followed. About 1490. Silverpoint. (*Windsor, #12317.*)

17. *Bust of a man, and an architectural study.* The study of the man is probably for the figure of St. James the Great in *The Last Supper*. About 1497. Sanguine. *(Windsor, #12552.)*

18. *Earthquake, fiery rain, resurrection of the dead, and other studies.* About 1500. Pen.
(Windsor, #12388.)

19. *Cartoon for "The Virgin with Saint Anne."* 75 x 50 cm. This shows notable variations with respect to the composition of the Louvre painting, for which the cartoon was almost complete in April 1501. However, this cartoon is probably somewhat earlier. Black crayon and white lead. *(London, Royal Academy.)*

20. *Head for the Saint Anne in "The Virgin with Saint Anne."* Still, this does not exactly correspond to either the Louvre painting or the cartoon in the Royal Academy in London. Executed in the early years of the sixteenth century. Pencil, with white lead highlights and the veil blue, on red-tinted paper. *(Windsor, #12534.)*

21. *Plant study*: *Sparganium erectum L.* Probably from the early years of the sixteenth century. Sanguine. *(Windsor, #12430 r.)*

22. *Plant study*: *Rubus Idaeus L.* Probably from the early years of the sixteenth century.
Sanguine. *(Windsor, #12419.)*

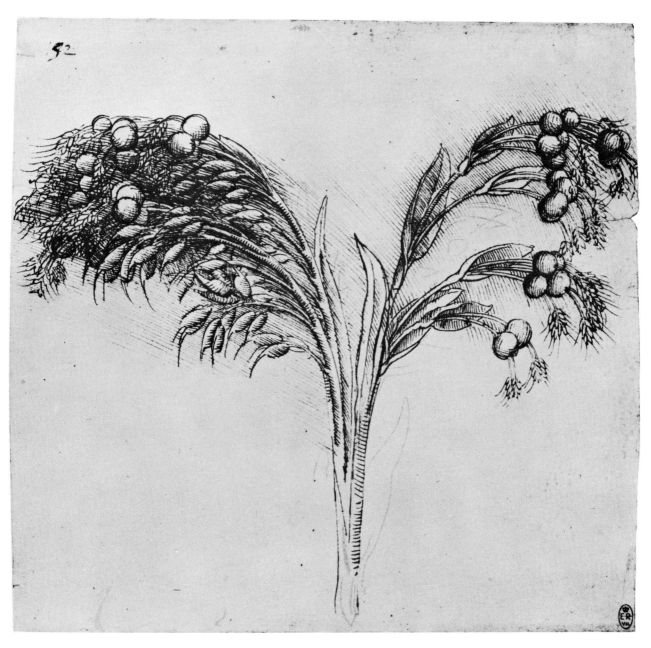

23. *Plant study*: *Coix Lachryma L.* Probably from the early years of the sixteenth century.
Pen. *(Windsor, #12429.)*

24(b) and (c). *Battle sketches for "The Battle of Anghiari."* 1503. Pen. *(Venice, Accademia, #215 v. and r.)*

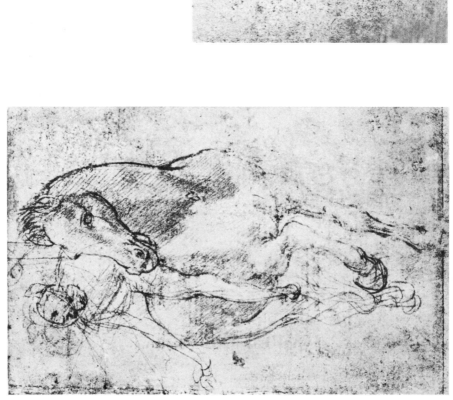

24(a). *Horse and rider.* Probably for the Uffizi *Adoration of the Magi* (1481), in which almost the identical figure appears in reverse in the background. Pen. *(Newport, R. I., Coll. J. N. Brown.)*

25. *Horses.* If, as it seems, this is a sketch for *The Battle of Anghiari*, it would be dated as 1503. Sanguine. (*Windsor, #12340.*)

26. *Study of horses, and head of a shouting man.* This used to be considered a sketch for the Uffizi *Adoration of the Magi* (1481), but the ferocious expressions of the horses, the head of the shouting man and the drawing of a horse on the back of the page all point to its being one of the first drawings for *The Battle of Anghiari* (1503). Pen, with a few brushstrokes. *(Windsor, #12326.)*

27. *Head of a young man.* Study for *The Battle of Anghiari*, 1503-104. Sanguine.
(Budapest, #343.)

28(a). *Poplar grove.* About 1500. Sanguine. *(Windsor, #12431 r.)*

28(b). *Rope-drawn ferry.* Like the Windsor drawings #12398 and #12999, it seems to me that Leonardo's inspiration for this came from the gorge at Trezzo, where the river Adda met the waters of the Grande Naviglio (a navigable canal). Probably drawn during the second Milanese period. Pen. *(Windsor, #12400.)*

29. *Storm in the mountains.* Probably inspired by the view from the basin of Lecco (with the town in the background, "le Grigne," etc.). From the last years of the first Milanese period, or else a resumption, in the second period, of analogous studies. Sanguine.
(Windsor, #12409.)

30. *Study of rocks.* Probably a resumption in the second Milanese period of the studies of mountains begun during the first period. Charcoal. (*Windsor, #12397.*)

31. *Design for Marshal Trivulzio's tomb monument.* Second Milanese period. Crayon.
(Windsor, #12354.)

32. *Cataclysm.* From the last decade of Leonardo's life. Black crayon. (*Windsor,* #12382.)

SUPPLEMENT

33. *Sketch for the hanging figure of Bernardo di Bandino.* Probably drawn from life. 1479. Pen. *(Bayonne, Musée Bonnat.)*

34. *Studies for a "Madonna of the Cat."*
The finest with this motif. About 1480.
Pen and wash. *(Florence, Uffizi, #421.)*

35. *Bust of a warrior*. Suggested doubtlessly by a figure in Verrocchio's *Beheading of the Baptist*. About 1480. Silverpoint on cream colored prepared ground. *(London, British Museum.)*

36. *Studies of an angel placing a shield on a trophy and separate studies of an angel.* About 1480-1481. Pen and brown wash over a drawing with a stylus. *(London, British Museum.)*

37. *Study of the perspective of the background of "The Adoration of the Magi."* About 1481. Pen over metalpoint with wash. *(Florence, Uffizi, #436.)*

38. *Allegorical composition.* Pleasure and pain represented as twins. 1483-1485. Pen
(Oxford, Library of Christ Church College.)

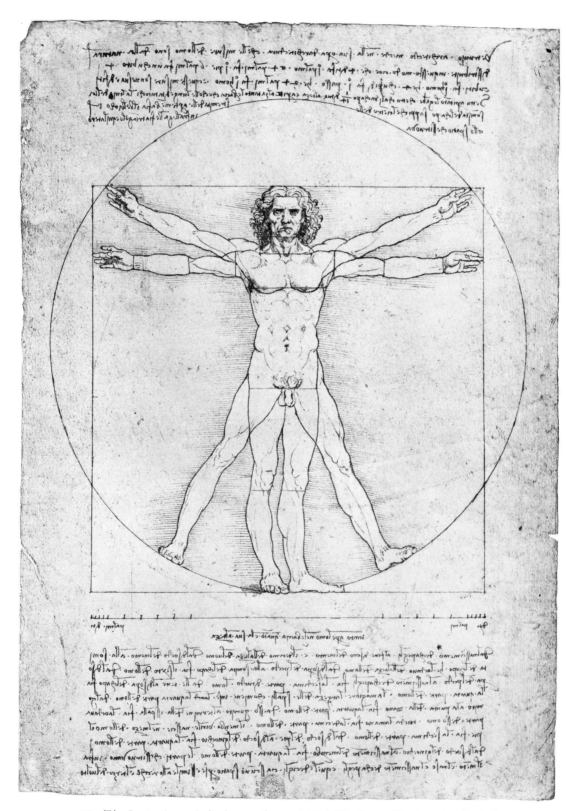

39. *The Proportions of the human figure.* 1485-1490. Pen. *(Venice, Accademia.)*

40. *Profile of a lady.* The workmanship has much in common with plate 12, but the pose anticipates the cartoon of Isabella d'Este. Silverpoint on pale pinkish ground. 1486-1488. *(Windsor, #12505.)*

41. *Nude on horseback trampling a prostrate foe.* For the monument to Francesco Sforza. About 1490. Silverpoint on blue prepared surface. (*Windsor, #12358.*)

42. *Studies for the Sforza monument.* About 1490. Leadpoint on prepared surface.
(Windsor, #12360.)

43. *Design for a stable*. Architectural drawing. About 1490. Pen. *(Paris, Institut de France.)*

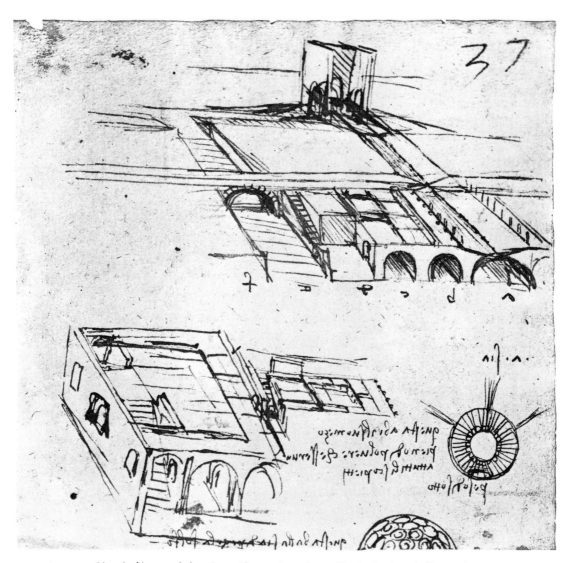

44. *Architectural drawing.* About 1490. Pen. *(Paris, Institut de France.)*

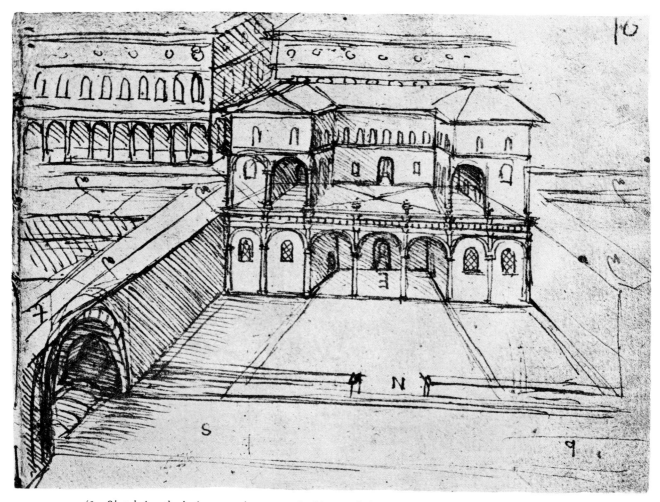

45. *Sketch for the laying out of a town.* Architectural drawing giving a partial view of a town with a double system of high and low level roadways. About 1490. Pen.
(Paris, Institut de France.)

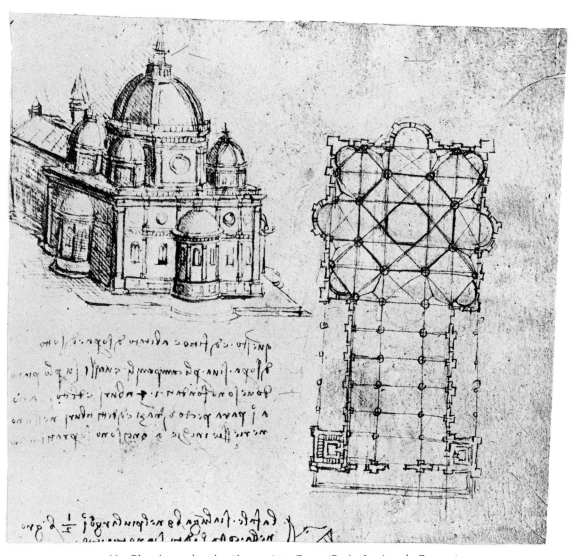

46. *Plan for a church.* About 1490. Pen. *(Paris, Institut de France.)*

47. *The unmasking of evil.* Sketch for an
allegory. About 1494. Pen over sanguine.
(Bayonne, Musée Bonnat.)

48. *Sketch for an allegory.* About 1494.
Pen over leadpoint. *(Paris, Louvre.)*

49. *Head of a man.* Probably a study for the head of Philip in *The Last Supper.* About 1497.
Black chalk. *(Windsor, #12551.)*

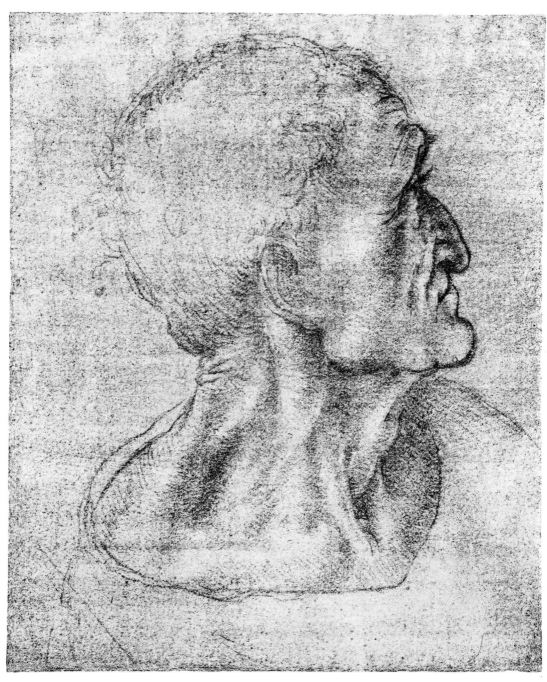

50. *Head of a man.* Study for the head of Judas in *The Last Supper.* About 1497. Sanguine.
(Windsor, #12547.)

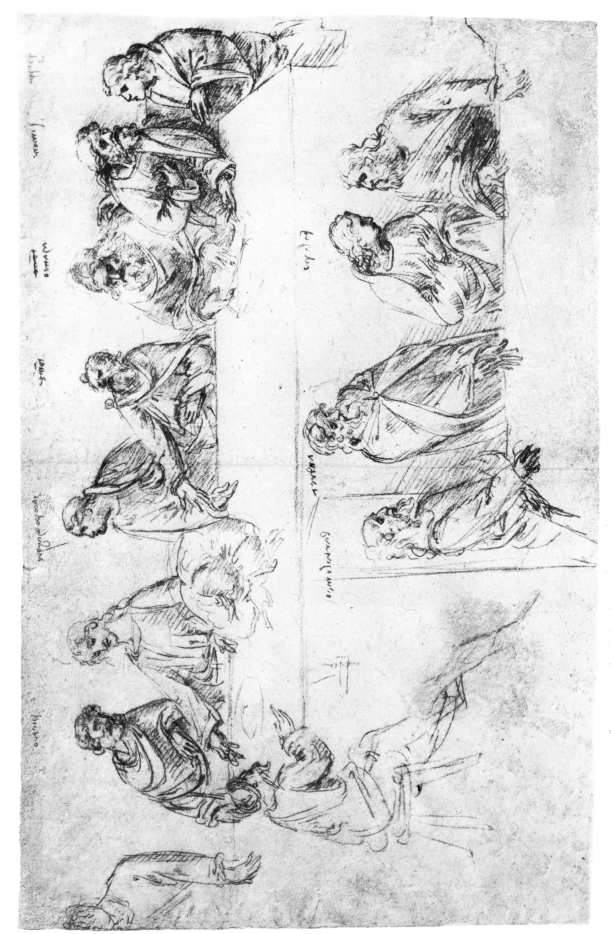

51. *Preparatory sketch for the painting of "The Last Supper." About 1497. Sanguine. (Venice, Accademia.)*

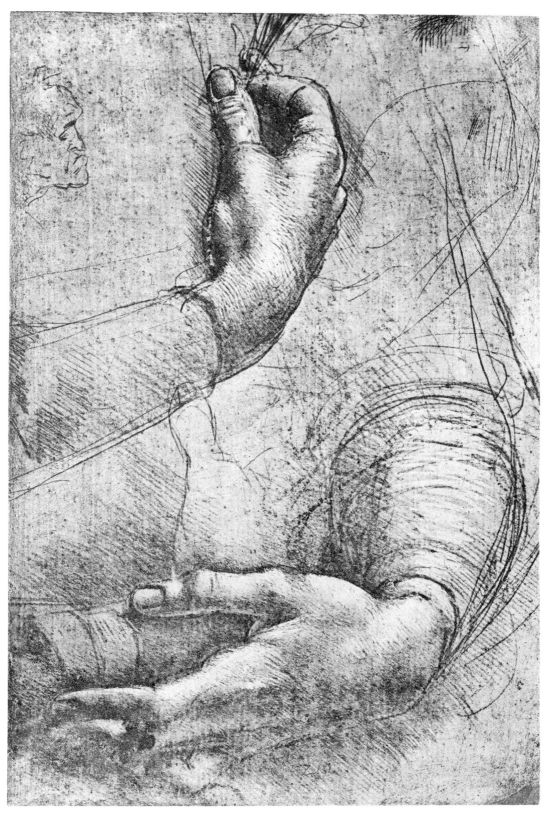

52. *Study of female hands.* The type of hand with its slender thin form is more like the style
of *The Virgin of the Rocks* than the *Mona Lisa.* Before 1500. Silverpoint heightened with
white. *(Windsor, #12558.)*

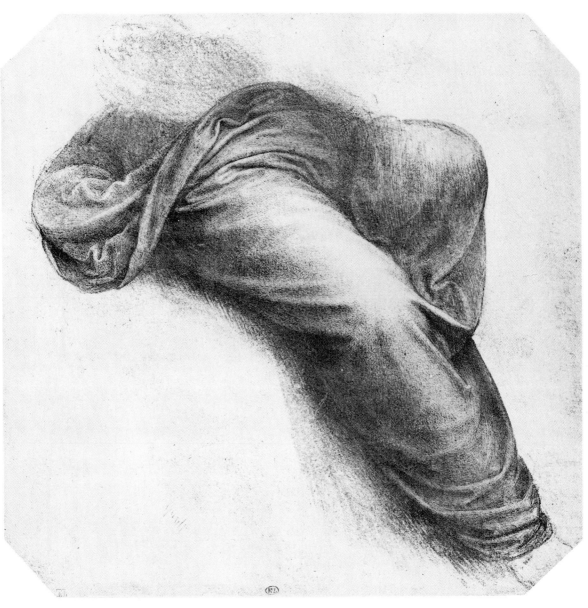

53. *Study of drapery.* A study for the Louvre version of *The Virgin with Saint Anne.*
Unfortunately the drawing is modernized but the original line is nearly untouched. About
1500. Black chalk, bistre wash and white. *(Paris, Louvre.)*

54. *Studies of the head of Cesare Borgia.* 1502. Sanguine. (*Turin, Royal Library.*)

55. *Warriors' heads.* Studies for the two central figures in *The Battle of Anghiari.* 1503-1504.
Black chalk and sanguine. *(Budapest, Museum of Fine Arts.)*

56. *Neptune guiding his sea horses.* Probably a study for the cartoon which Vasari said was designed for Antonio Segni. 1503-1504. Black chalk. *(Windsor, #12570.)*

57. *Study from the antique.* Head of youth in profile. About 1504. Sanguine. Hair touched with black chalk. *(Windsor, #12554.)*

58. *Studies of dancing nymphs.* 1504-1508. Pen. (*Venice, Accademia.*)

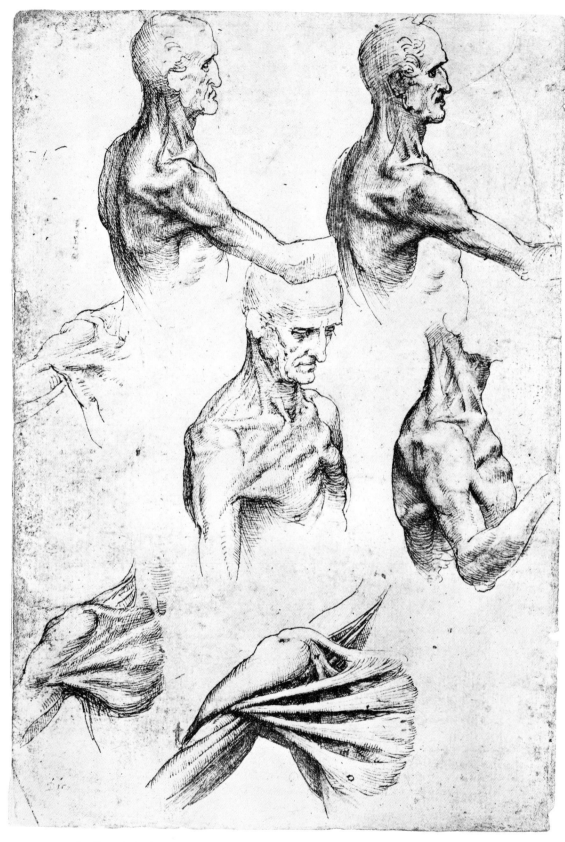

59. *Studies of the head and shoulders of a man.* Anatomical drawing. 1510. Pen, washed
with india ink. *(Windsor, #19001.)*

60. *Allegory.* The wolf sitting in the stern of the boat probably represents the church; the eagle with the crown hovering over him is probably the Empire; the globe, the earth. About 1510. Sanguine on brownish-grey paper. (*Windsor, #12496.*)

61. *Youth with a lance.* After 1513. Pen and wash over black chalk. *(Windsor, #12575.)*

62. *Sketches for a kneeling Leda and a horse.* The outline and pen strokes point to Leonardo's last years. Black chalk. The Leda is gone over with a pen. *(Windsor, #12337.)*